READY, SET, LAUNCH YOUR BUSINESS

A 21-STEP GUIDE TO ASSIST WITH LAUNCHING YOUR BUSINESS

DR. SYNOVIA DOVER-HARRIS

Ready, Set, Launch Your Business. A 21-step guide to assist with launching your business

Copyright © 2017 by Dr. Synovia Dover-Harris
Printed in the United States of America

First Printing
ISBN 978-1-943284-18-4 (pbk.)
ISBN 978-1-943284-19-1 (ebk)

A2Z Books, LLC
Lithonia, GA 30058
www.A2ZBooksPublishing.com
Manufactured in the United States of America
A2Z Books Publishing has allowed this work to remain exactly as the author intended, verbatim.

INTRODUCTION

It is 9 pm on Sunday night, and I just walked in from the 4th day of renovations on my new business venture, which is a gym. For over a year, one of my business partners/personal trainer/nutritionist and I have been thinking about collaborating with this new young gym owner to diversify our portfolio as well as jump into the gym business. I started my very first business when I was 5 years old. I had a name, a hand-drawn logo (before I knew anything about computers), and even a tagline. I used to go with my mom in the mornings to drop my grandmother off at work and sometimes we would stop at this store that sold meat (I guess this was when people purchased their meat from meat markets and not grocery stores). But the main thing I liked about the store and was always interested in was the Candy Bars and not just any Candy Bars, but the Good Candy Bars like Snickers and Kit Kat (I knew about picking quality product since the beginning). I was a weird kid because I did not like candy very much and still do not until this day, but something clicked in me and said buy these four .25 candy bars with that dollar you have and sell it. I bought them, took them to school with a ribbon and a handmade tag and sold them for 50 apiece. I remember doing that for the first time and being instantly hooked on business and the art of selling. That was my very first business and the beginning of everything for me. Since then, I have started and assisted with starting for myself, my clients, and my students because I teach entrepreneurship at the University level; hundreds of companies. And what I have learned along the way is that most of us take way too much time to launch our companies. For one reason or another, most of us move slowly because we are either afraid or do not know what steps to take. Now, granted; it does take years to build a successful brand and business. However, with the right strategy and plan of action, a business can be successfully launched in a matter of days. Hi, I'm Dr. Synovia Dover-Harris, and I am going to give you the tools, you need to get your business running with these 21 Steps in Ready, Set, Launch your Business.

The most important step in starting a business is getting started....

HOW TO USE THIS GUIDE

This guide contains 21 Steps to Assist With Launching your Business. All of the steps are action items that you will need to complete and will assist you with starting your business successfully and within a timely manner. This book can be utilized to launch any type of company, and most of the steps should be easy to complete and implement. However, because this is a resource guide, assistance may be required.

You will need:

- An allocated place to work.
- At least 30/45 minutes to complete each step (some may require more, and other may require less).
- A computer/tablet or cell phone (to conduct research).
- Something to write on (notebook/journal/word doc).
- Something to write with (pen/pencil).
- A calendar or scheduling system of some sort to create timelines/deadlines.

The steps/action items are strategically designed to align and propel you in the right direction to starting your company...

READY...

SET...

LAUNCH YOUR BUSINESS!

CONTENTS

Step 1
What & Why

Step 1 is identifying what type of business you are starting. You need to ask yourself; who you are, what are you passionate about and why are you starting this business? You need to ask yourself these questions because your answers will determine how you need to strategize to build the business and the brand.

Are you the type of person who loves to cook or someone that loves to work out? If you love to cook, then starting a catering company may be a good fit and if you love to work out, then becoming a personal trainer or opening a gym might be a business for you. On the other hand, if you dislike working out, then becoming a personal trainer may not be the best business for you.

Additionally, you need to answer why you are starting this business. People are known to start businesses to:

- ✓ Earn Extra Income.
- ✓ Become Self-Employed.
- ✓ Earn Credibility, Respect, & Trust.
- ✓ Create Jobs and Opportunities.

Answer the following:

- ✓ What are you passionate about?
- ✓ What kind of business are you starting and what do you want to be known for?
- ✓ What product and/or service will you provide and what problem are you solving?
- ✓ Where will your business be ran? At a Venue or Online?
- ✓ How much will it cost to start and how will you obtain the financing?

Take the Next 60 minutes and answer
What Business are you Starting & Why...

USE THIS AREA TO WRITE
NOTES ABOUT YOUR BUSINESS

_____

_____

_____

_____

_____

_____

_____

_____

_____

_____

_____

_____

_____

_____

Step 2
It's all in a Name

Step 2 is identifying your Business Name. Your Business "Name" is the single most important thing you will have. Your Business name is what your company will go by from now until the end of time. Therefore, taking the time and careful consideration when creating your Business Name is vital.

Your Business name will tell your consumers who and what you are and what you represent. Apple has nothing to do with computers. However, Steve Jobs came up with the name Apple because he gave his employees one day to think of a good name. Otherwise, he said he would put the company name A for Apple. He got many names at the end of the day, but did not like any of them, as a result, the next day he named his company Apple (who else would be so lucky?) Google came from the word "googol", which was a term created by then a nine-year-old named Milton Sirotta who was the nephew of the American mathematician Edward Kasner. Research shows that Kasner asked his nephew to create a name for a very large number and Milton called it a googol. The term was later made popular and in Kasner's book, *Mathematics and the Imagination*, which he co-authored with James Newman. Later, another mathematician invented the term "googolplex," which represents ten to the power of a googol - a substantially larger number.

Take the next 30 minutes and Research Business Naming Strategies...

Ask yourself:

- ✓ Do I want a catchy or trendy name or something classic and conservative?
- ✓ Will my business be named after someone? Or will it be named after me?
- ✓ Will my business name have something to do with the products and services my company is providing?
- ✓ Will my business name be self-explanatory or will my consumers have to figure out what I do?

What is the name of my Business and Why?

USE THIS AREA TO WRITE
NOTES ABOUT YOUR BUSINESS

Step 3
Paperwork

Step 3 is obtaining your legal paperwork. Now that you have chosen a business name, it is time to obtain your legal paperwork. Every type of business needs some form of license or permit to operate legally and varies per state.

Take the next 45 minutes and Research the following ...

- ✓ Reserving your name (To stop anyone else from using it).
- ✓ Registering your business (LLC, Corporation, S-Corp, Etc.).
- ✓ Obtaining an EIN.
- ✓ Obtaining a Business License (If applicable).
- ✓ Obtaining a Seller's Permit (If applicable).

Reserving your name and registering (LLC, Corporation, Etc.) your business shows that you are a legal functioning business. Your name and business registration can be completed at the Secretary of State website for your state. The entity choice should be based on your individual business needs.

The EIN# also known as the TAX ID # is like a social security number for your business and is needed to open a business bank account, merchant services, and pay business taxes if applicable. The EIN# can be obtained through the IRS.GOV website, but the registration should be completed first. If you are selling products, you will need both a business license and a seller's permit.

Conduct some research and decide if you want to obtain your paperwork on your own, or you can contact your small business administration office, a business consultant, a lawyer, or someone you know that can answer the questions for you and assist with obtaining your paperwork.

What paperwork do I need and how will I obtain them?

USE THIS AREA TO WRITE
NOTES ABOUT YOUR BUSINESS

Step 4
Products/Services

Step 4 is deciding and identifying what you are selling. To be successful in business, you must master the art of selling, and you must provide the right product or service better than your competition.

You should sell:
- ✓ What you like and have a passion for.
- ✓ What you would buy.
- ✓ Something that solves a problem.
- ✓ Something that is marketable and is in demand.

Take the next 45 minutes and answer the following:

- ✓ What is your product/service?
- ✓ Do you have a passion for this product/service?
- ✓ Describe your product/service?
- ✓ Would you buy this product/service and use it yourself?
- ✓ Are you excited about this product/service?
- ✓ Will your product or service be sold on location or online?
- ✓ Do you have a background or credential needed to provide this product or service?
- ✓ Would you sell this to your friends/family members etc.?
- ✓ What are your pricing strategy and price points?
- ✓ How will your product/service be fulfilled?
- ✓ What special software, equipment, supplies or technology is required to provide your product or service?
- ✓ What is the future products/service that can be created?
- ✓ How long can you sell this product or service?

What are your product/services?

USE THIS AREA TO WRITE
NOTES ABOUT YOUR BUSINESS

_____

_____

_____

_____

_____

_____

_____

_____

_____

_____

_____

_____

_____

_____

Step 5
Packaging

Step 5 is creating a packaging strategy. Service packaging is just as important as product packaging, so you need to decide how you will package your product/services to sell to your target audience.

Many start-ups make the mistake of choosing the wrong packaging, and this will instantly turn off your customer. People are stimulated by visuals, and to attract your customer, your packaging needs to be immaculate. Your packaging should be created based on your target market (see Step 17 for target market) and encompass your company's vision, mission, & unique value proposition (See Step 16).

Your packaging is your products/service outfit. Therefore, everyone will see an outfit that does not fit correctly. Packaging should be lightweight and compact, but be appealing, innovative, provide a massive impression, but simple to use for the end user.

Deciding on packaging requires time, money and effort. Therefore, to get this right, the following is required:
- ✓ Research (design & styles).
- ✓ Hire a good package/virtual content designer.
- ✓ Make sure colors, shapes, material choices, and font encompass your company and product.
- ✓ Good pricing.
- ✓ Knowing how your packaging will be stored.
- ✓ Quantity limits required to purchase.
- ✓ Consider transportation mode (if you have to mail etc.).

Additionally, incorporate things like barcodes and built in visibility to the package design.

Take the next 30 minutes and answer
What will your packaging look like, who will create it, and is it feasible for your product?

USE THIS AREA TO WRITE
NOTES ABOUT YOUR BUSINESS

_____

_____

_____

_____

_____

_____

_____

_____

_____

_____

_____

Step 6
Merchant Services/Banking

Step 6 is having a merchant service or business bank account. As a new business owner, you may be wondering how you would establish a business bank account and what other services will you need. You may also be asking yourself, do you really need a merchant service or business bank account, but unless you are a cash only business, which is highly unlikely, you will need a business /merchant service account so that you can accept credit card payments and operate as a legit business.

There are many options that you can choose from. However, the choice should be made based on the type of services and offers the bank will provide and the fees associated with that company. Also, fees add up, so it is essential to factor those in. There are companies like First Data, PayPal, Stripe, Square, and Apple pay, or you can talk to your current bank provider (Wells Fargo, Bank of America, etc.) and see what offers they have for new small business owners with business bank accounts and merchant services.

You can visit the bank or call, and here is a list of questions to ask the business bank merchant services account provider before making a decision:

1. What are the banking fees?
2. Do you provide 24-hour support?
3. Will you assist with business banking and set up?
4. Do I have to be PCI Compliant (Research this term)?
5. Is there a contract and/or termination fee if I leave?

Once you have chosen your payment system, make sure that you can take payments via online (website, landing pages, etc.), tablet, & smartphone, etc. The more ways you can accept payments, the more ways you have to make money. No one wants to have to search for how to pay you.

Take the next 60 minutes and research
business bank accounts and merchant services and choose one.

USE THIS AREA TO WRITE
NOTES ABOUT YOUR BUSINESS

_____

_____

_____

_____

_____

_____

_____

_____

_____

_____

_____

_____

_____

_____

Step 7
Accounting/Bookkeeping

Step 7 is organizing your financials. As a new small business, you want your financials to be organized, and this is why accounting for a Small Business is very important. For one, you want to keep track of all of your transactions rather it be accounts payable (money going out) or accounts receivable (money coming in), and you need to keep track of all of your transactions and not just for your records but also for tax purposes. As a new small business, you can do something as simple as a Microsoft spreadsheet, or you can purchase accounting software like QuickBooks or Wave and get started very easily. Or you can hire a CPA or business accountant and let them handle all of this.

Do the following:

- ✓ **Decide on your accounting system:** Will you use cash accounting or accrual accounting. Cash Accounting is like balancing your checkbook. Monies that come in is recorded, monies that go out is also recorded, and balance is created. Accrual accounting is when revenues and expenses are documented when the actual transaction occurs (even if the cash isn't in or out of the bank yet) and requires tracking receivables (monies coming in) and payables (monies going out).
- ✓ Track Expenses
  - o Meals
  - o Travel
- ✓ Calculate your Gross Margins (research).
- ✓ Determine how you will be paid (20% of net).
- ✓ Set up a Payroll system (if applicable).

Take the next 45 minutes and Research
Accounting Systems and choose one.

USE THIS AREA TO WRITE
NOTES ABOUT YOUR BUSINESS

_____

_____

_____

_____

_____

_____

_____

_____

_____

_____

_____

_____

_____

_____

Step 8
Brand Strategy

Step 8 is creating a Brand Strategy. A brand strategy is a long-term formal plan created by setting branding goals, identifying the brand's message, and then creating the steps to accomplish those goals. Creating a branding strategy can be a difficult task and sometimes confusing if you do not know a lot about branding (Ready, Set Build your Brand is available), but is definitely needed to launch a successful business.

Ask yourself:

- ✓ What is the purpose of my business? For example: My business was created to help businesses and business professionals properly brand themselves in the marketplace.
- ✓ What do I want to accomplish as a brand? For example: I want to help businesses and professionals identify their brand in an attempt to build successful businesses to attain wealth.
- ✓ How will I accomplish these branding goals? For example: I will take 2 hours a day to work on creating my brand, marketing via social media, and ensuring that I am assisting my clients effectively.

Some Branding Goals that should be identified are:

- Defining your brand's principles.
- Building the brand awareness.
- Creating a trustable and credible brand.
- Identifying how to attract and convert customers.

Take the next 45 minutes and research and create a Brand Strategy...

USE THIS AREA TO WRITE
NOTES ABOUT YOUR BUSINESS

_____

_____

_____

_____

_____

_____

_____

_____

_____

_____

_____

_____

_____

_____

Step 9
Brand Message

Step 9 is defining a brand message. The brand message will explain to your consumers why you are in business in the first place, as well as explain to the world what you do and how. Additionally, your brand message is your brand's voice, which means it is speaking for you. Brand messages come in many forms and includes things like the sales pitch; the colors chosen, the logo, as well as the taglines and slogan. A brand's message is the expression of the brand through words. Nike's Message/Slogan is "Just Do it" meaning get it done. Apple's Message/Slogan is "Think Different" which means be innovative.

You can determine your Brand's Voice/Message by answering the following questions:

- ✓ What is it that your brand is saying and how? (For example: Let's get healthy. My brand is speaking through ads, social media, & testimonials).
- ✓ Who are you saying it to and what does it sound like? (For example: Women ages 18 to 25 & it sounds inspirational).
- ✓ What is your Brand's language based on?(For example: Staying fit & gaining clients).

Here are some Tips to creating a Brand Message:
1. Create an outline.
2. Test the reaction of others.
3. Make sure your message is:
   a. Clear
   b. Consistent
   c. Competitive

Take the next 30 minutes and create your Brand's Message.

USE THIS AREA TO WRITE
NOTES ABOUT YOUR BUSINESS

_____

_____

_____

_____

_____

_____

_____

_____

_____

_____

_____

Step 10
Brand Image

Step 10 is defining your brand's image. Your brand image is what your target audience will see and perceive your company as and what they will think of when they think of your company. Your brand's image should be created to reflect the brand's personality and should always reflect positivity. A brand's image can be developed once the brand knows what it wants to sound and look like and is usually developed over a period and consists of a company's:

- ✓ Logo (Should be professional and memorable).
- ✓ Color (Choose colors that reflect the brand's persona).
- ✓ Websites (Create a website that provides pertinent information).
- ✓ Marketing Materials (Create marketing materials that reflect to the brand).
- ✓ Social Media and all online presence (Create Facebook, Instagram, and Twitter pages and often post on your brand's products and services, but ensure that the content posted are professional and shows the brand in a positive light.

When you chose your brand image, make sure it represents what you are trying to relay in your visuals. All of your marketing materials, business social media post, and even your wardrobe should tie into your brand's image.

To hone in on your business image answer the following question-
- ✓ How do I want to be perceived by my consumers?
- ✓ What do I want them to think about when they see my brand?

Take the next 30 minutes and identify your Brand's Image?

USE THIS AREA TO WRITE
NOTES ABOUT YOUR BUSINESS

_____

_____

_____

_____

_____

_____

_____

_____

_____

_____

_____

_____

_____

Step 11
Business Logo

Step 11 is designing your company's logo, which is a part of Step 10; the brand's image. A logo is very significant and is just as important as the name of your company. The business name is what the business will go by. The brand's message is the voice of the brand. So, the business logo is the face of the brand and is what everyone sees and will be the number one representation of the company.

A logo is defined as a graphical symbol, mark, emblem, and sometimes-even words that are utilized to represent a company.

The famous Nike swoosh stands for speed and motion and needs little explanation since Nike is the #1 multinational sports company in the world. The Mercedes logo is a three-point Star that represents a dominant power over the land, sea, and air. Which is what Mercedes Benz claims that it does (I agree since I own one).

When creating a Business/Brand logo ask yourself the following:
- ✓ What will my logo say about my company?
- ✓ What will people think when they see my logo?
- ✓ What do I want people to feel when they see my logo?

Here are 3 Tips to creating a Brand Logo:
1. Be Unique.
2. Pick Colors and Fonts that represent your Company.
3. Make it understandable.

You can create your logo (not recommended unless you are a graphic artist) or hire someone to do it for you. You can spend a few hundred dollars as I did for my very first logo I got created from a local graphic artist or $49 as I did for my second logo from a company I found online or even $5 on Fiverr. As long as it is professional and represents your brand, you will be fine.

Take the next 30 minutes and order your Logo Today!

USE THIS AREA TO WRITE
NOTES ABOUT YOUR BUSINESS

_____

_____

_____

_____

_____

_____

_____

_____

_____

_____

_____

_____

_____

_____

_____

_____

_____

_____

_____

_____

_____

_____

_____

_____

_____

Step 12
Business Website

Step 12 is creating your company's website. Everything about you, your company, and/or your business should be found on your website. Consumers should never have to guess what it is that you do or figure out how to find you. Or are you one of those individuals who send potential clients to your Instagram or Facebook pages? Do not get me wrong; Social media is very important. However, DO NOT make the mistake of not having a website in addition to your social media pages. Facebook, Instagram, Linkedin, Twitter, Snap Chat and all the other social media platforms are all great tools for marketing your company; however, these are not professional platforms to display your business. When consumers see your products and/or services on social media, this is to engage and entice them to want to know more, and this is when you should send them to your website.

Your website should display:

- ✓ What your company does.
- ✓ How your product/service is a benefit to the consumer.
- ✓ How you can be contacted.

Additionally, your website should be:

- ✓ Visually stimulating.
- ✓ Informative, but succinct.
- ✓ A great representation of your business.
- ✓ Mobile friendly.
- ✓ Grammatically correct.

Once your website is completed: Ask yourself: What does my website say about my Company and Brand?

- ✓ Does it say that your company is innovative and with the times? Or does your website display your company as stagnant and boring? If you are unsure, when completed, take a poll by asking friends, family members, and colleagues what they think.

You can create your website on platforms likes: WordPress, Square Space or Wix or you can hire someone to do it for you.

Take the next 60 minutes and research website designs!

USE THIS AREA TO WRITE
NOTES ABOUT YOUR BUSINESS

_____

_____

_____

_____

_____

_____

_____

_____

_____

_____

_____

_____

_____

Step 13
Social Media

Step 13 is setting up your social media pages. Depending on your age, you may or may not be interested in social media; however, if you want to reach a vast amount of your consumer no matter what age, you need to set up social media business accounts. I recommend a business page and/or group on Facebook, a business page on Instagram, and even a twitter page.

You can join a company like **Hootsuite or Planoly** that will allow you to schedule your posts if you feel as, though you do not have time every day to post to these sites. Additionally, on Hootsuite, you can schedule the same post on multiple platforms at the same time.

Social Media Stats

There are:
- ✓ 30 million monthly active Instagram users.
- ✓ Almost 2 billion active monthly Facebook users.
- ✓ 313 million active monthly Twitter users.
- ✓ 500 million active monthly Likened users.

Therefore, how can you be in business and not be on social media?

If you do not have content to post, then you should strategize on obtaining content. If you provide consulting services, then you can post consulting tips. If you are a chef, then you can post recipes. If you are a personal trainer, you can post exercises, meal plans, and things of that nature. Remember when building a brand, people will buy you before they buy your product/service. Therefore, when you post, make sure your potential clients get a good picture of who you are and what problem your business is solving.

Set up your accounts today. Use your logo as your profile pictures and start building your social media presence. Post often and post with a purpose.

Take the next 60 minutes and Set Up your Social Media Sites!

Social Media Posting Example

	Facebook	Twitter	LinkedIn	Pinterest	Google+
Minimum	3 X per week	5 X per week	2 X per week	5 X per day	3 X per week
Maximum	10 X per week	none	5 X per week	10 X per day	10 X per week

Business Tip: Start A Business you would want to Run even if you Never made any money.

USE THIS AREA TO WRITE
NOTES ABOUT YOUR BUSINESS

_____

_____

_____

_____

_____

_____

_____

_____

_____

_____

_____

_____

_____

_____

_____

_____

_____

_____

_____

_____

_____

_____

_____

_____

Step 14
Building your team

Step 14 is planning your human resources. Now that you have your products/services, branding strategy, and paperwork done (or at least started), now it is time to plan your human resources.

When I first started my company, I did everything on my own because I could not afford to hire anyone. However, I learned very quickly that it is almost impossible to run a business successfully without a team. I found myself being the consultant, the editor, the graphic artist, the marketing person, the administrative individual and everything else. Once I hired a few people to help me with a few things, my business soared because instead of spending all my time doing everything under the sun, I could spend my time gaining new clients and offering a spectacular product and service.

If you are new to business and do not have a lot of financials to hire individuals, you can still outsource for a fraction of the cost; meaning hire on an as-needed basis and only use them when you need them. Having an IT person over marketing is not good, so make sure whomever you hire is well versed and specialize in the area you need assistance in. On another note, you can even barter with friends or family members. You can do something for them and have them to assist you with things like accounting, or marketing, or whatever you need help with.

Take the next 30 minutes and Answer the following questions:

- ✓ Will I be operating my business on my own?
- ✓ Who can help me build my business?
- ✓ Will I be hiring individuals myself? If so, who and for what part of the business?
- ✓ Where will I find my help? Will they be interns, full or part-time employees? Will they be contractors and hired on an as-needed basis?
- ✓ What will be their responsibilities?
- ✓ What will be my hiring processes? What will I be paying them and how? When will I start the hiring process?

Step 15-21 is Business Planning in which we will cover the Steps to Creating a Business plan. A business plan is needed because it is a roadmap to your future.

Remember a failure to plan is a plan to fail!
-Walter Myers

Business Tip:

Market your products/services at all times.

Step 15
Executive Summary

Step 15 is the first section of a Business plan, which is an Executive Summary.

The Executive summary is the most important part of a business plan and is the first (and sometimes the only) thing the reader will read, and although, we are creating it first, it will not be finalized until the business plan is completed. The Executive Summary is simply a brief review of the business plan that will let the readers know at a glance what is in the business plan.

Take the next 30 minutes and research Executive Summaries …

Use the following to write your Executive Summary:
- ✓ Describe the start-up process and background of your company.
- ✓ Describe your organizational structure.
- ✓ Provide where, when and why you started the business.
- ✓ Provide where you are located and why.
- ✓ Provide your objective with this venture.
- ✓ Provide your related background and experience.

Executive summaries should:
- ✓ Make sense.
- ✓ Be informative but succinct.
- ✓ Be written for the target reader.
- ✓ Define the problem your business will be solving.
- ✓ Use graphics, bullets points, and headings.

Write your Executive Summary.

USE THIS AREA TO WRITE
NOTES ABOUT YOUR BUSINESS

_____

_____

_____

_____

_____

_____

_____

_____

_____

_____

_____

_____

_____

_____

_____

_____

_____

_____

_____

_____

_____

_____

_____

_____

Step 16
Vision statement, mission statements, and the Unique Value Proposition

Step 16 is writing your vision statement, mission statement, and the unique value proposition of your company.

A **vision statement** is a statement that provides where the company wants to be and includes the goals, objectives, and aspirations. A vision statement is what the world looks like after you have finished changing it and should be what you return to whenever you get confused about your business goals.

A **mission statement** is a statement that will describe the business features and philosophies. A mission statement will be the organization's core values and the reason for existing.

A **unique value proposition** is a statement that defines the benefits your company offers that is unique and different from your competition.

Take the next 45 minutes and research Vision Statement, Mission Statements, and Unique Value Propositions...

For example:

Google's vision statement is to provide access to the world's information in one click.

Google's mission statement is to organize all of the data in the world and make it accessible for everyone in a useful way.

Google's UVP is its deep understanding of the relationship between users and web content. Whether this is search and results or targeted advertising, Google can connect the two better than anyone else.

Write your vision statement, mission statement, and unique value proposition.

USE THIS AREA TO WRITE
NOTES ABOUT YOUR BUSINESS

Step 17
Target Market

Step 17 is identifying your company's target market.

A target market is a group of customers a business has decided to aim its marketing efforts and is a group of people considered likely to buy a product or service. A target market consists of customers that share similar characteristics, such as:

✓ Age.
✓ Ethnicity.
✓ Income.
✓ Lifestyle.

For example: The target market for Ready Set Launch Your Business book is lower to middle-class men and women ages 21 to 45 who want to launch a business and might have some college.

Take the next 30 minutes and research Target Markets...

Note: A well-defined target market is needed because it helps with allocating marketing resources.

Your Company's Target Market is determined by answering who will want your products and/or services through the following questions:

✓ Who is your customer (Men, Girls, Companies, etc.)?
✓ What do they look like (18-25, 60 & up, African Americans or Small start-up companies)?
✓ What do they do (College students, retired, & sell products)?
✓ Where can you find them? (Universities, Retirement homes, Instagram, etc.)

Who is your target market?

USE THIS AREA TO WRITE
NOTES ABOUT YOUR BUSINESS

Step 18
Market Analysis

Step 18 is conducting a market analysis. A market analysis studies the real marketplace of your business.

Take the next 30 minutes and research Market Analysis ...

You might be asking yourself why I need a market analysis. The reason is, you do not want to start a business, and you do not know the market or industry. Have you ever went to a store and asked someone a question about a product/service and you could instantly tell that they are only there for a paycheck? If the answer is yes, then you know this is not how you want to be perceived in your business. You want to know the ins and outs of your industry and the trends as well as the do's and don'ts.

Studying your industry and gaining as much knowledge about it is vital.

Answering the following questions will provide you with your Market Analysis.

- ✓ Describe your market /industry.
- ✓ What is the industries target market (This can be the same or different from your business target market)?
- ✓ Clarify the Market Needs.
- ✓ Is the Market Viable (If Yes, How Do You know)?
- ✓ What are the Potential Market Growth and Trends?
- ✓ What studies, statistics, and market test that have been conducted in your industry and what does it say?
- ✓ Do you need any training or education in the industry?

Conduct your Market Analysis.

USE THIS AREA TO WRITE
NOTES ABOUT YOUR BUSINESS

_____

_____

_____

_____

_____

_____

_____

_____

_____

_____

_____

_____

_____

Step 19
SWOT Analysis

Step 19 is completing a SWOT Analysis. A SWOT Analysis is an evaluation of your company to determine the business strategy based on where your company will stand in the actual industry

Take the next 30 minutes and research A SWOT Analysis ...

A SWOT Analysis involves the collection and portrayal of information about internal and external factors, which have or may have an impact on the business.

▶ **S,** which is for Strengths are the elements that give your company an edge over your competitors. *(For example, I provide an innovative process of launching a business for my clients).*

▶ **W,** which is for Weaknesses are the elements that can be risky if used against your company by your competitors. *(For example, I am a small printing company with few staff members; therefore, our publishing turnaround time is longer than larger publishers).*

▶ **O,** which is for Opportunities are positive conditions that can bring a competitive advantage to your company. *(For example, because I am a small printing company with not a lot of clients we offer one on one individualized assistance that cannot be captured by a bigger company. So we have the opportunity to offer better customer service/).*

▶ *T,* which is for Threats are negative conditions that can negatively affect your business. *(For example, I am a small printing company with not a lot of staff, so we are unable to take on a lot of clients at one time, and the competition can put us out of business).*

Conduct your SWOT Analysis.

USE THIS AREA TO WRITE
NOTES ABOUT YOUR BUSINESS

_____

_____

_____

_____

_____

_____

_____

_____

_____

_____

_____

Step 20
Competitive Analysis/Advantage

Step 20 is conducting your company's Competitive Analysis and identifying your Competitive Advantage. A competitive Analysis is the evaluation of the competition to identify their strengths. A Competitive Advantage is the strengths of your company that allows you to outperform your competition.

Take the next 45 minutes and research Competitive Analysis & Competitive Advantage ...

Knowing where your company sits on the market will assist in creating a competitive advantage. Every business has competition. Understanding the strengths and weaknesses of your competition--or potential competition--is critical to making sure your business survives and grows. While you do not need to hire a private detective, you do need to thoroughly assess your competition on a regular basis even if you only plan to run a small business. In fact, small businesses can be especially vulnerable to competition, especially when new companies enter a marketplace.

<u>Answer the following questions:</u>

- Who are your competitors and what are they doing? *(For example, Apple is the competitor of Samsung, and they offer innovative electronics.)*

- What are your competitor's weaknesses and can your company play off of that? *(Samsung is just as innovative, but are at a fraction of the cost).*

- What makes you or your company different? *(Samsung has products that are indestructible and waterproof. Apple does not).*

- What would make a customer choose your company's products and services over another? *(If you buy a Samsung over an Apple you can get just as good a product for a fraction of the costs).*

Conduct your Competitive Analysis.
What is your Company's Competitive Advantage?

USE THIS AREA TO WRITE
NOTES ABOUT YOUR BUSINESS

_____

_____

_____

_____

_____

_____

_____

_____

_____

_____

_____

Step 21
Marketing Strategy

Step 21 is creating the Marketing Strategy. The Marketing Strategy is a comprehensive plan that includes the marketing goals of a company.

Take the next 30 minutes and research Marketing Strategy ...

You will answer the following:
- ✓ What is your marketing budget?
- ✓ How will you position your products and services for your target customers?
- ✓ How will you use your unique value proposition to market to your target customers?
- ✓ How will you keep the customer engaged and retain them once you have them?
- ✓ How will you get leads?
- ✓ How will you expand your marketing in the future?
- ✓ What types of marketing will you use?
  - o Direct Mailing (flyers, postcards)?
  - o Door to Door?
  - o Internet marketing?
  - o Social Media?
  - o Referrals?
  - o Commercials?
- ✓ Will you hire marketing help or do it on your own?
- ✓ How often will you market? Daily, Weekly, Monthly, Quarterly and what types of campaigns will you run?
- ✓ Will you have branding/marketing materials:
  - o T-shirts?
  - o Hats?
  - o Or other branding material? If so where are they coming from?

Create your Marketing Strategy!

USE THIS AREA TO WRITE
NOTES ABOUT YOUR BUSINESS

_____

_____

_____

_____

_____

_____

_____

_____

_____

_____

_____

_____

_____

_____

_____

Step 22
Bonus Day

Put together your actual business plan with everything you've done over the past 7 days, and by now the website and all paperwork should be done.

Now it's time to:

Ready, Set, Launch Your Business.

Letter from the Author:

Congratulations on completing this 21 step guide to assist with launching your business. I commend you for making the first steps and working diligently to getting to this point. As a business consultant/coach for almost two decades, I have seen over the years that the hardest part of entrepreneurship is getting started. Most people do not know where or how to get started, so I decided to put together this guide to assist you with the process. Completing this book and all the necessary steps is just the beginning of the entrepreneurship journey. Use this guide as a resource even after you have completed your 21 steps. Always remember to plan often and plan with a purpose when it comes to your business. Stick with it and know that the sky is the limit.

Thanks,
Dr. Synovia Dover-Harris

Contact Info
Dr.Synovia@A2ZBookspublishing.com
Facebook/Synovia Dover-Harris
Instagram @Dr.Synovia

Order online at amazon.com and all other online distributors

Also Available:

Ready Set Build your Brand

Ready Set Write your Book

Coming Soon:

Ready Set Launch your Private Label

Ready Set Build your Team

Interested in Writing and or Publishing a BOOK???

Visit: www.A2ZBooksPublishing.com

www.ingramcontent.com/pod-product-compliance
Lightning Source LLC
Chambersburg PA
CBHW071723210326
41597CB00017B/2567